Bubbie Baby

Monica Hughes
Illustrated by Lisa Smith

Rigby®
A Harcourt Achieve Imprint

www.Rigby.com
1-800-531-5015

Bobbie has a farm.
The baby wants to play.

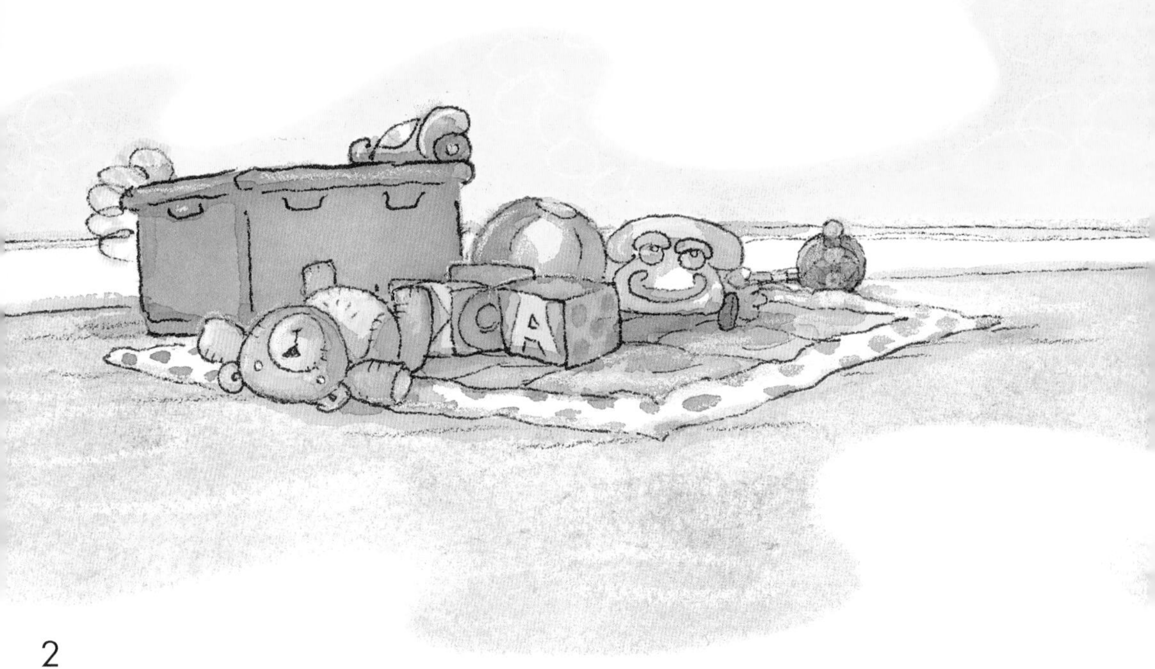

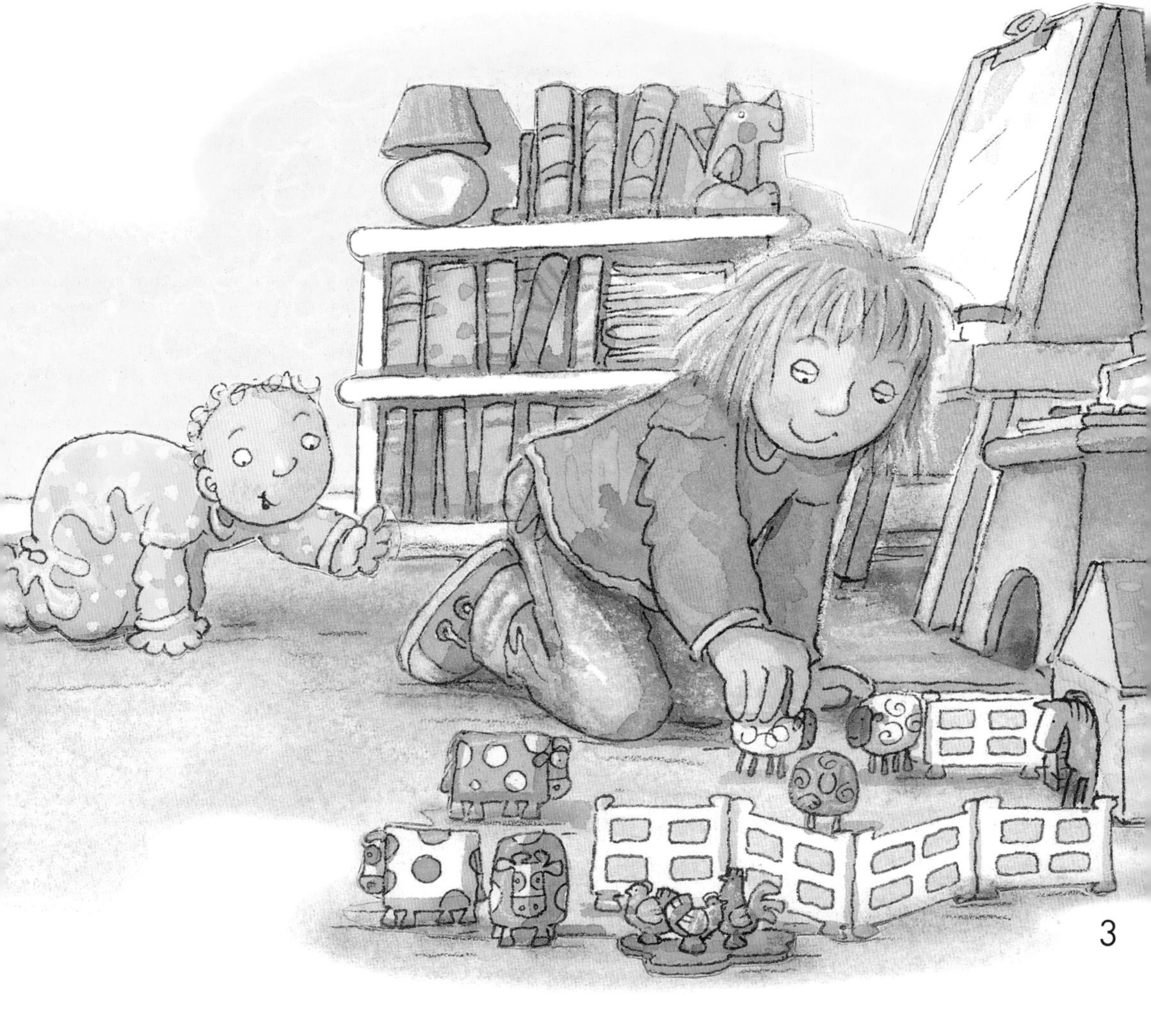

Bobbie says, "Go away, baby! Go away!"

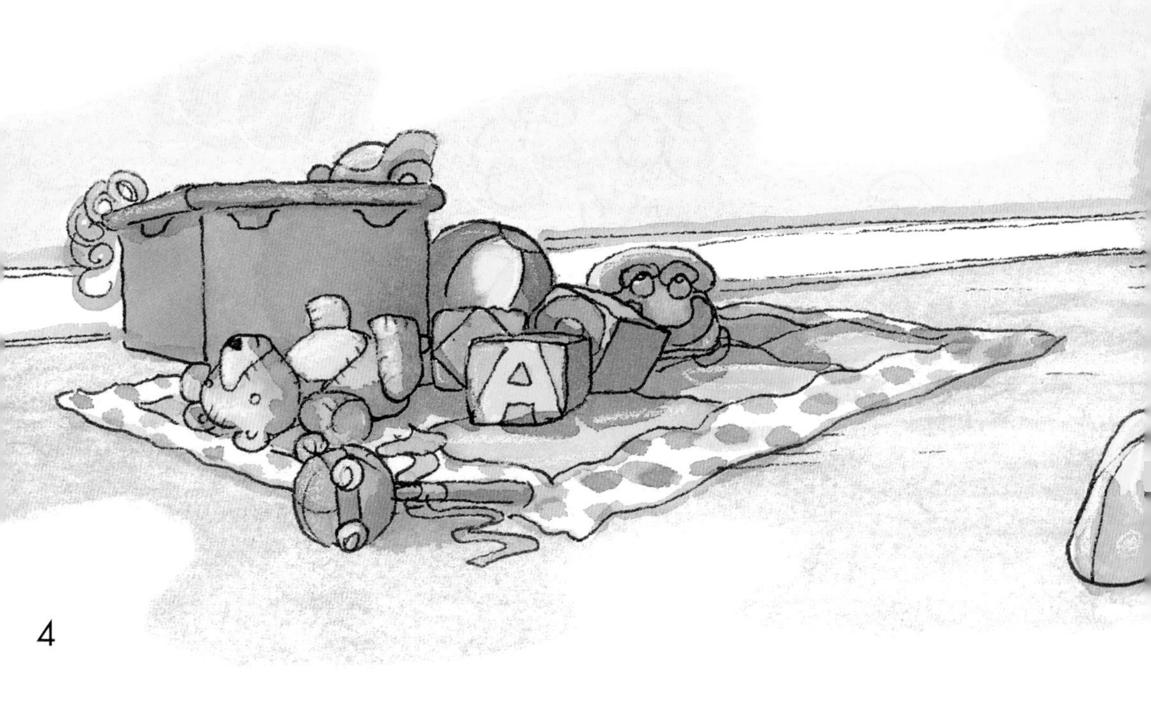

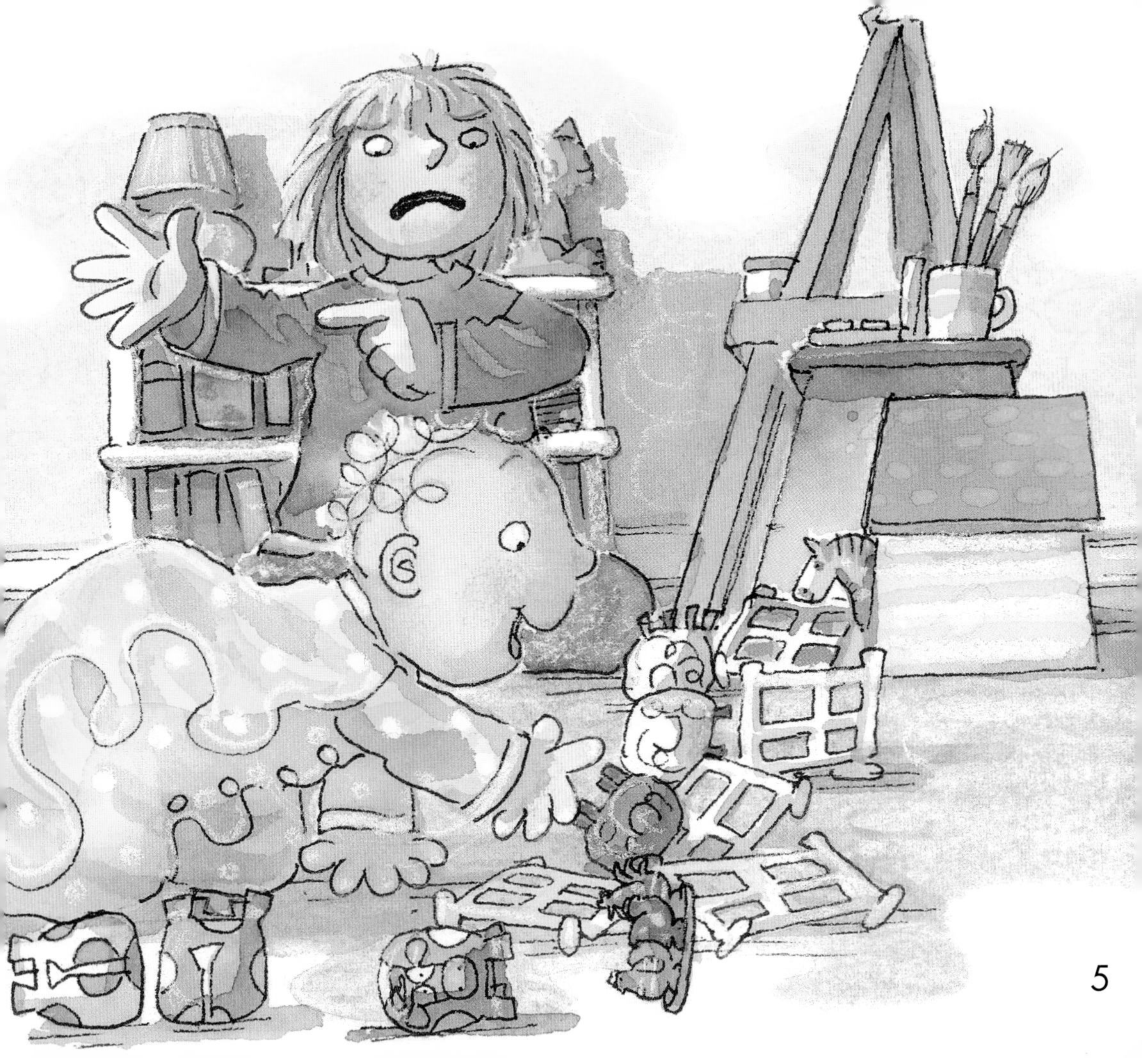

Bobbie has a train.
The baby wants to play.

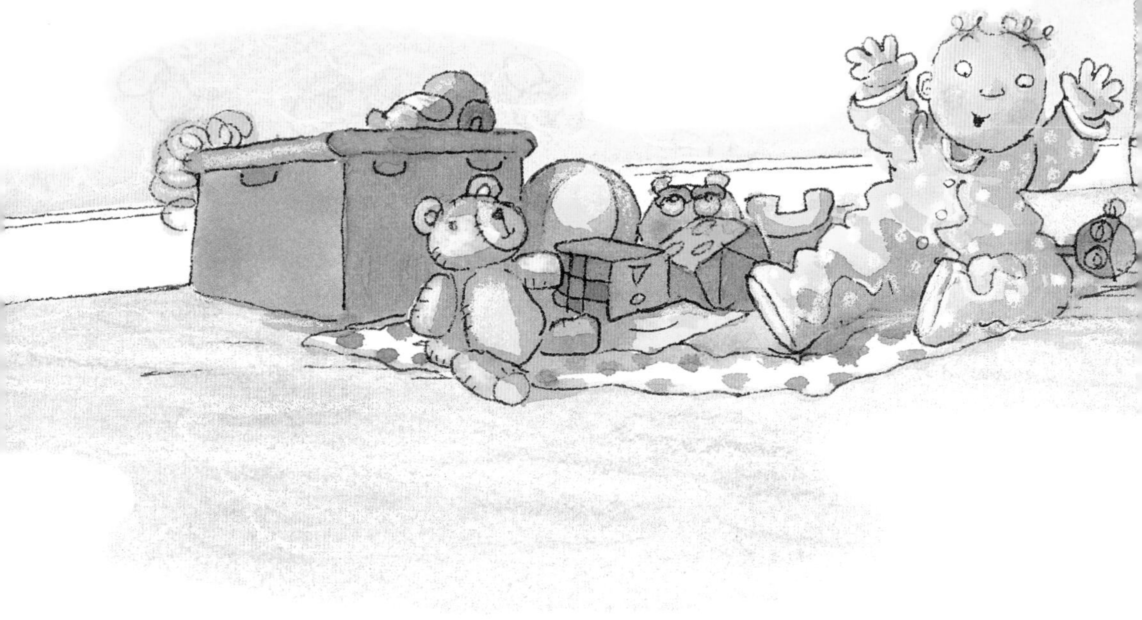

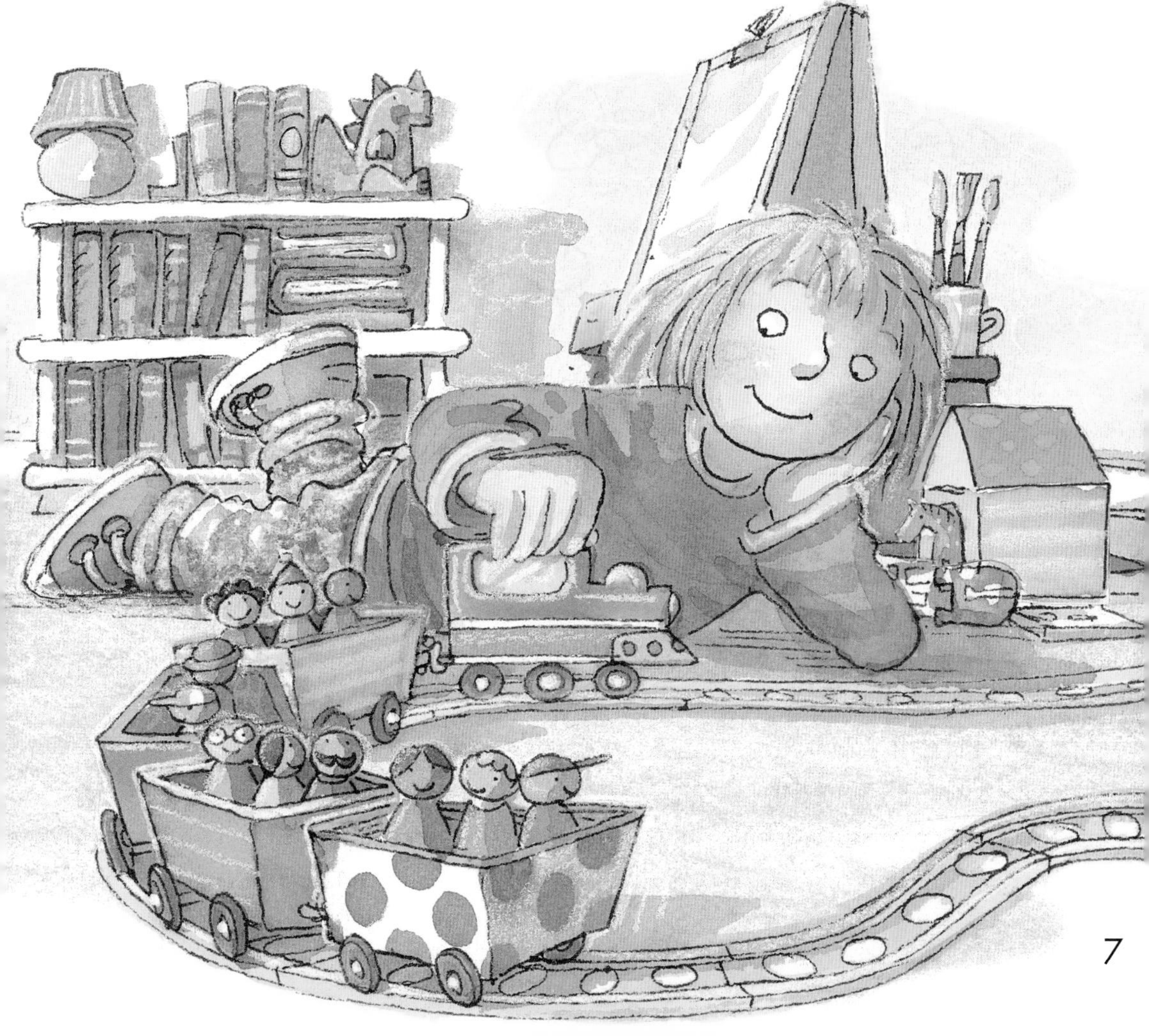

Bobbie says, “Go away, baby!
Go away!”

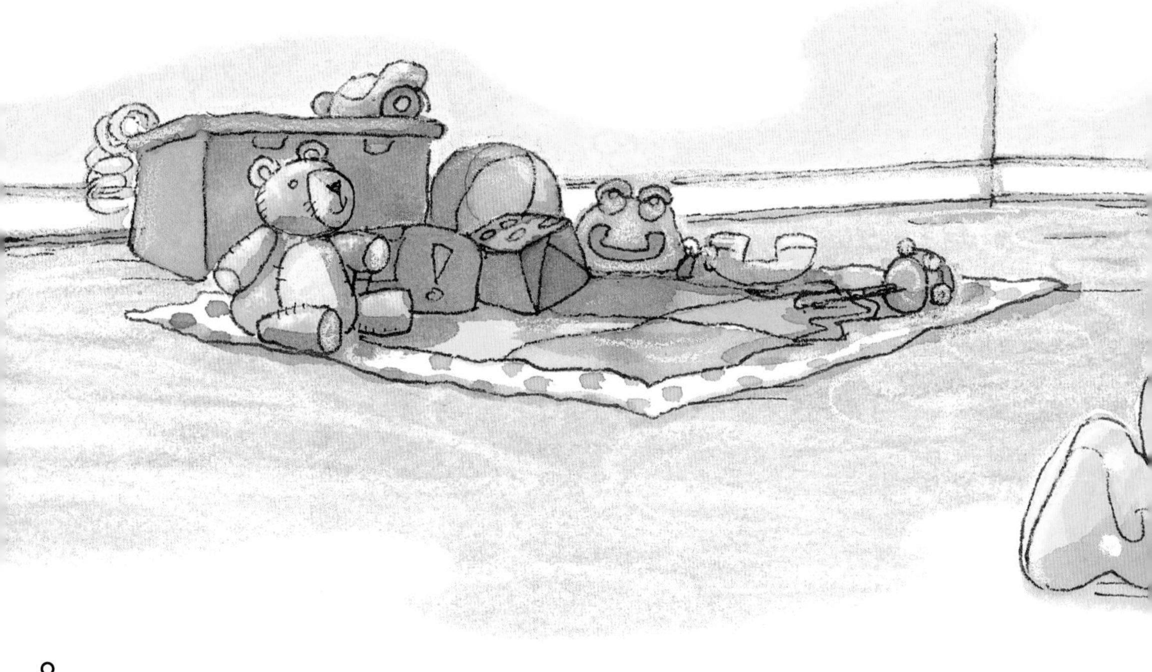

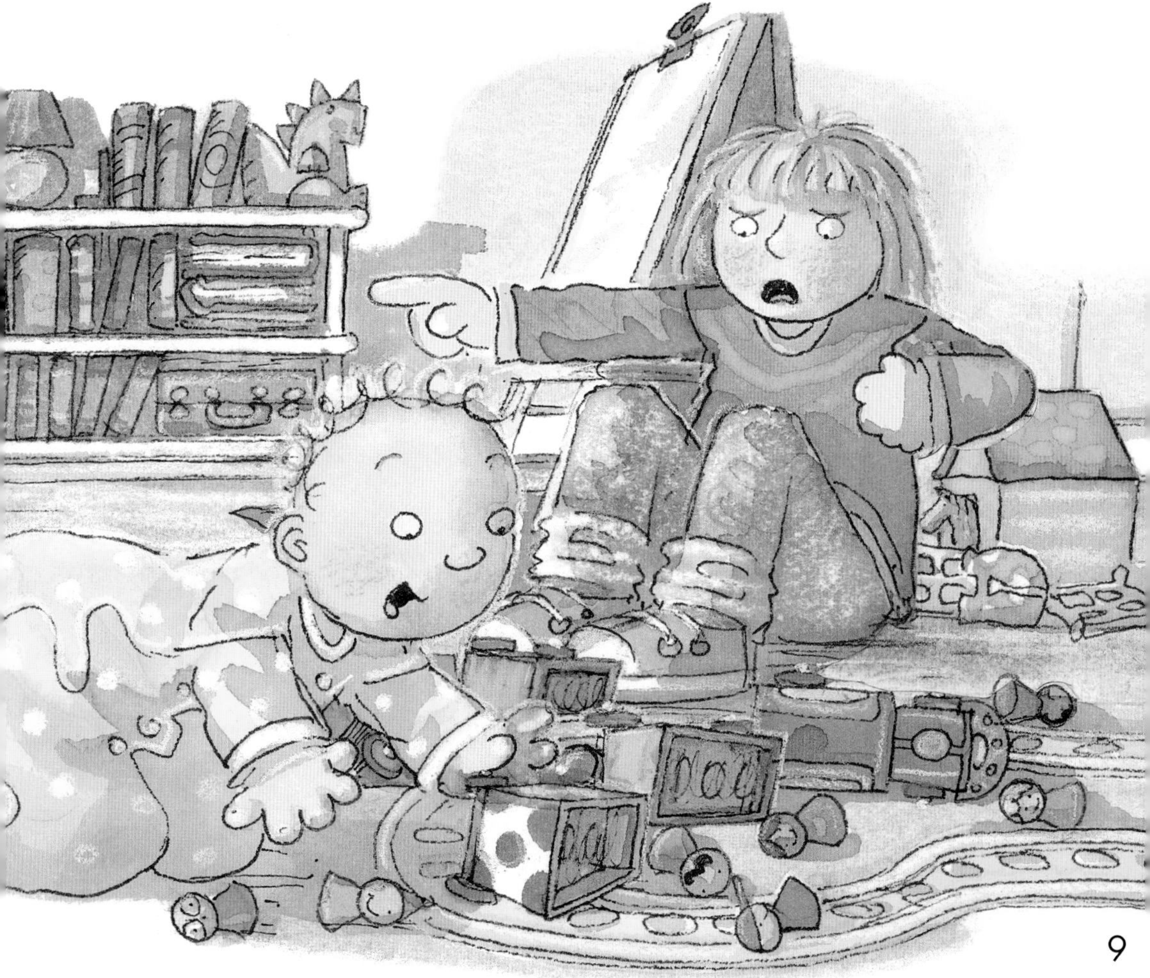

Bobbie has some paints.
The baby wants to play.

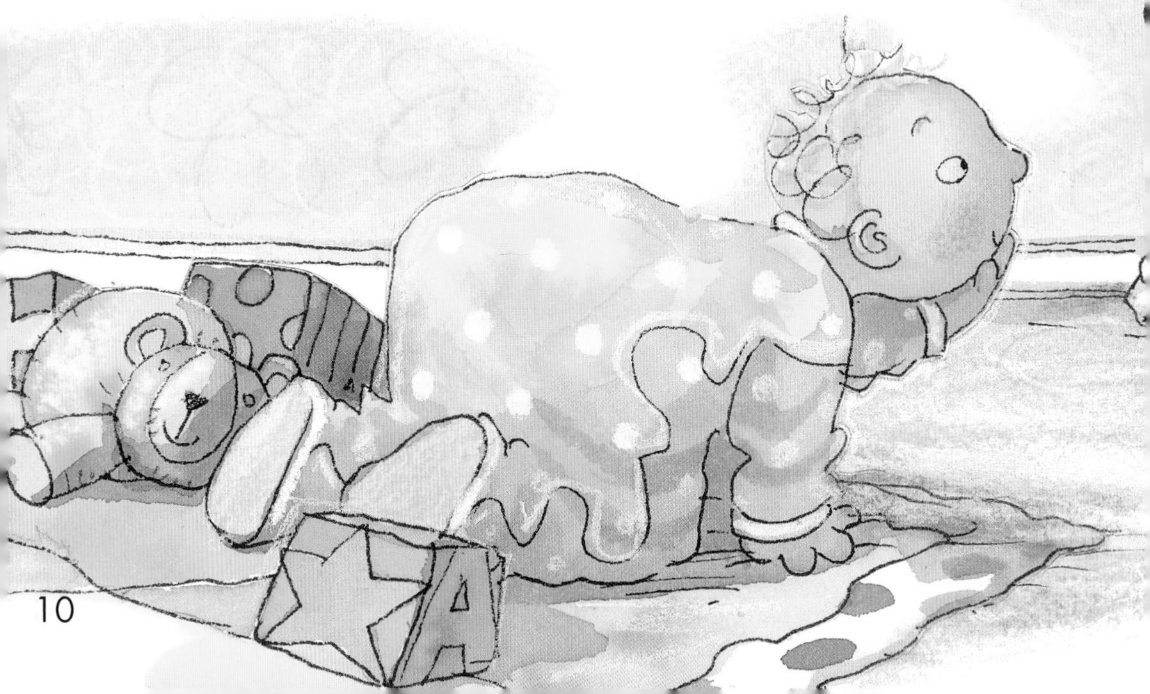

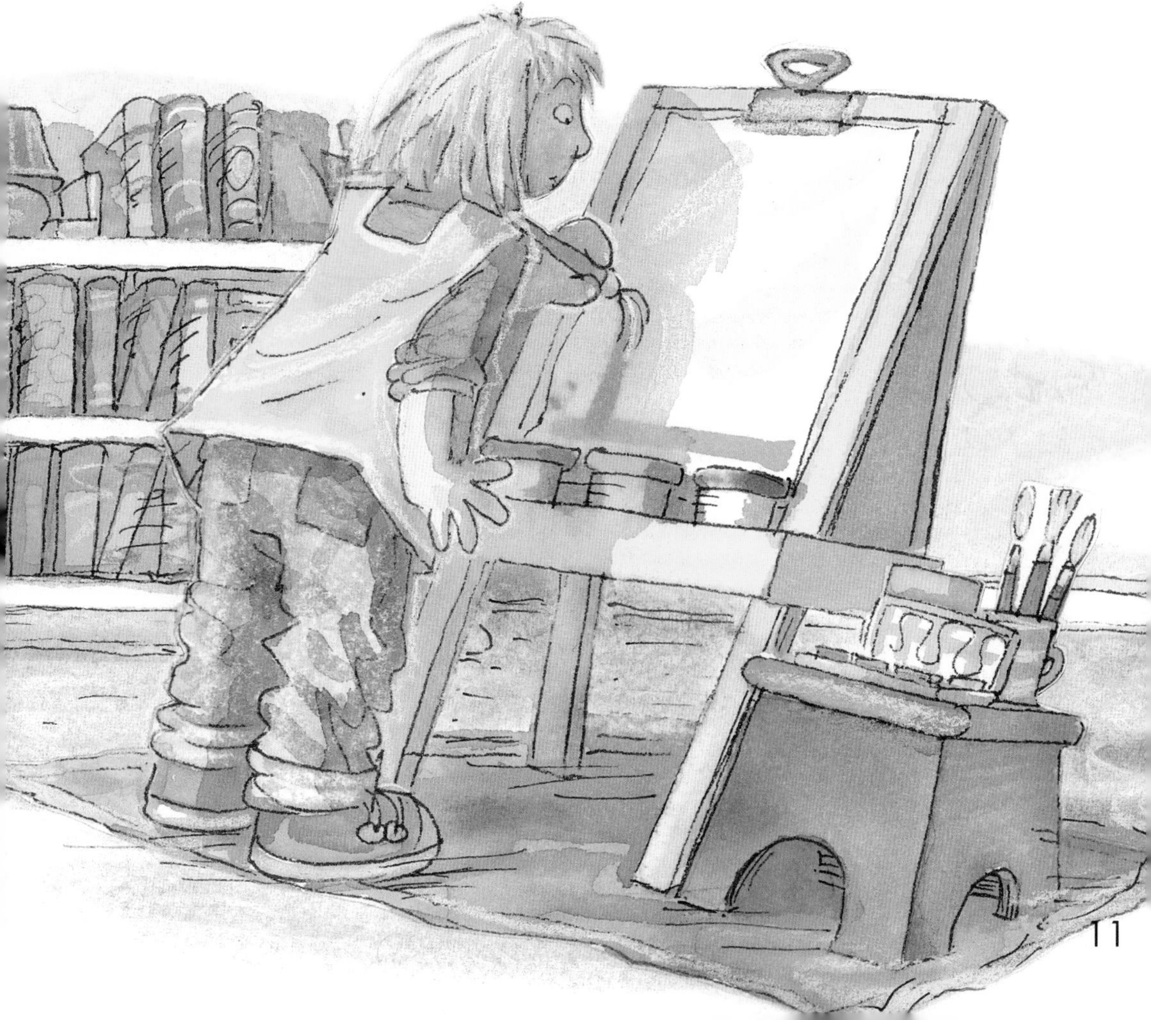

Bobbie says, “Go away, baby! Go away!”

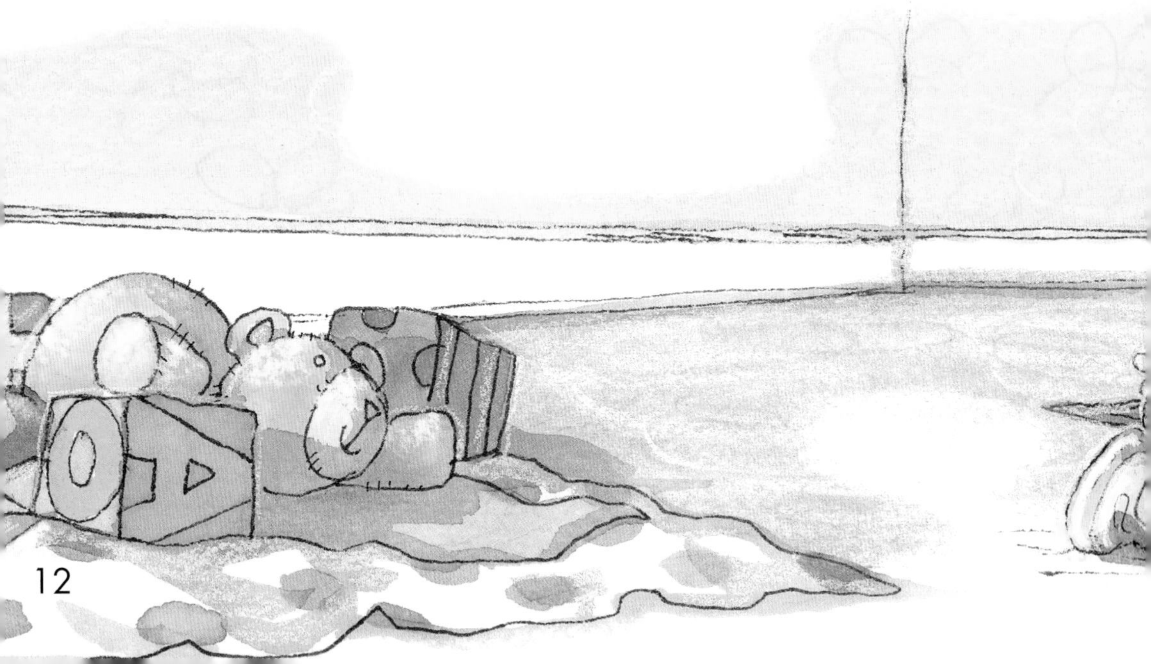

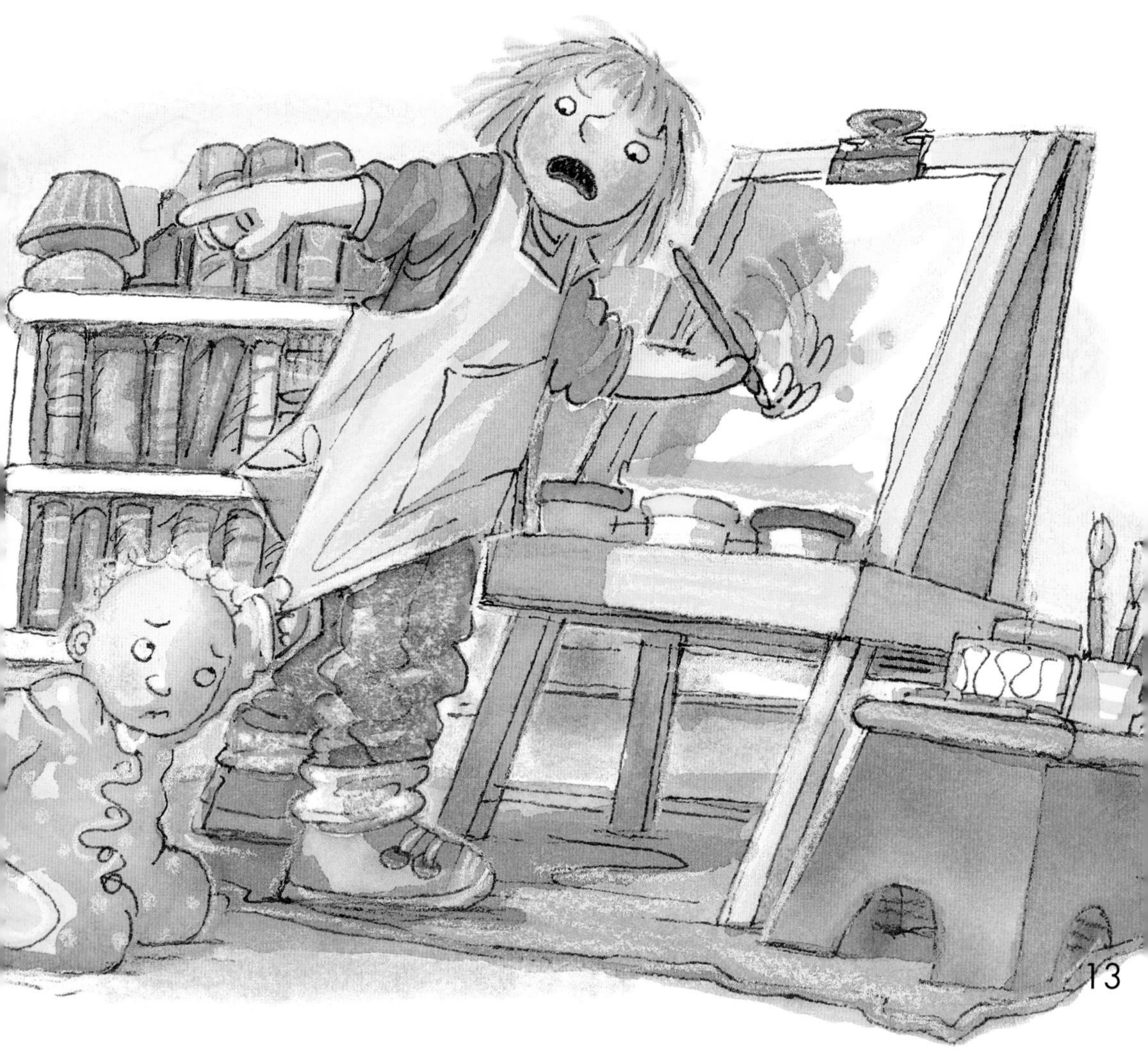

Bobbie has a book.
The baby wants to look.

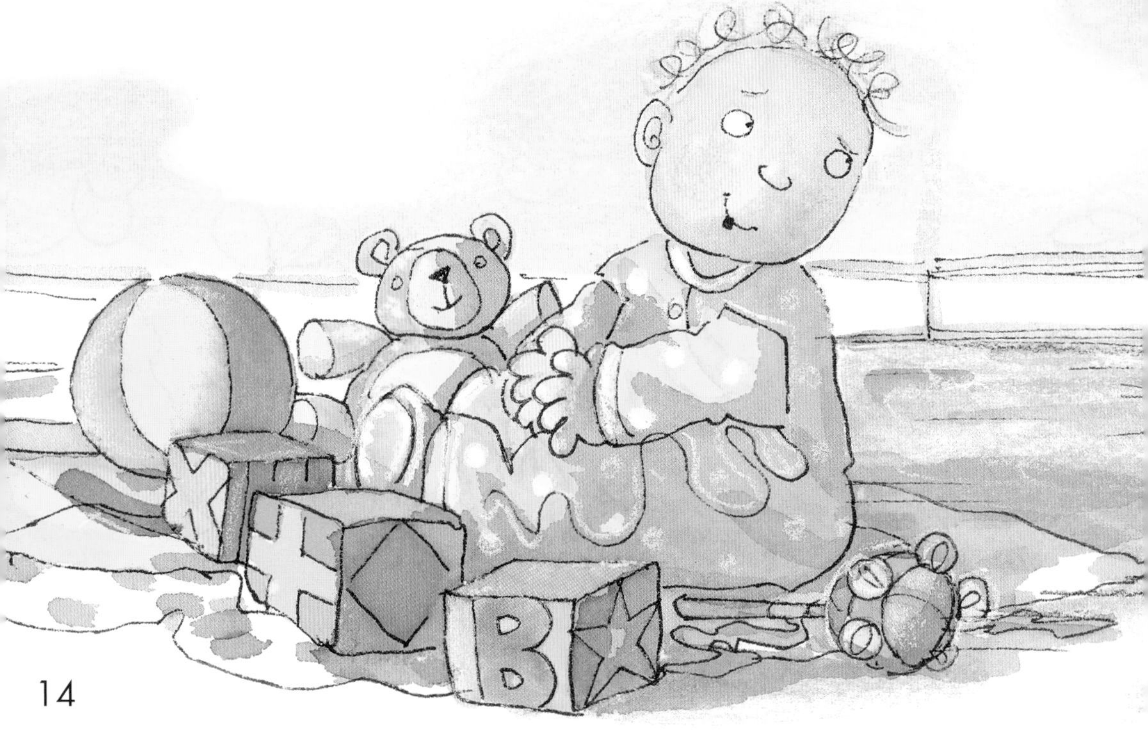

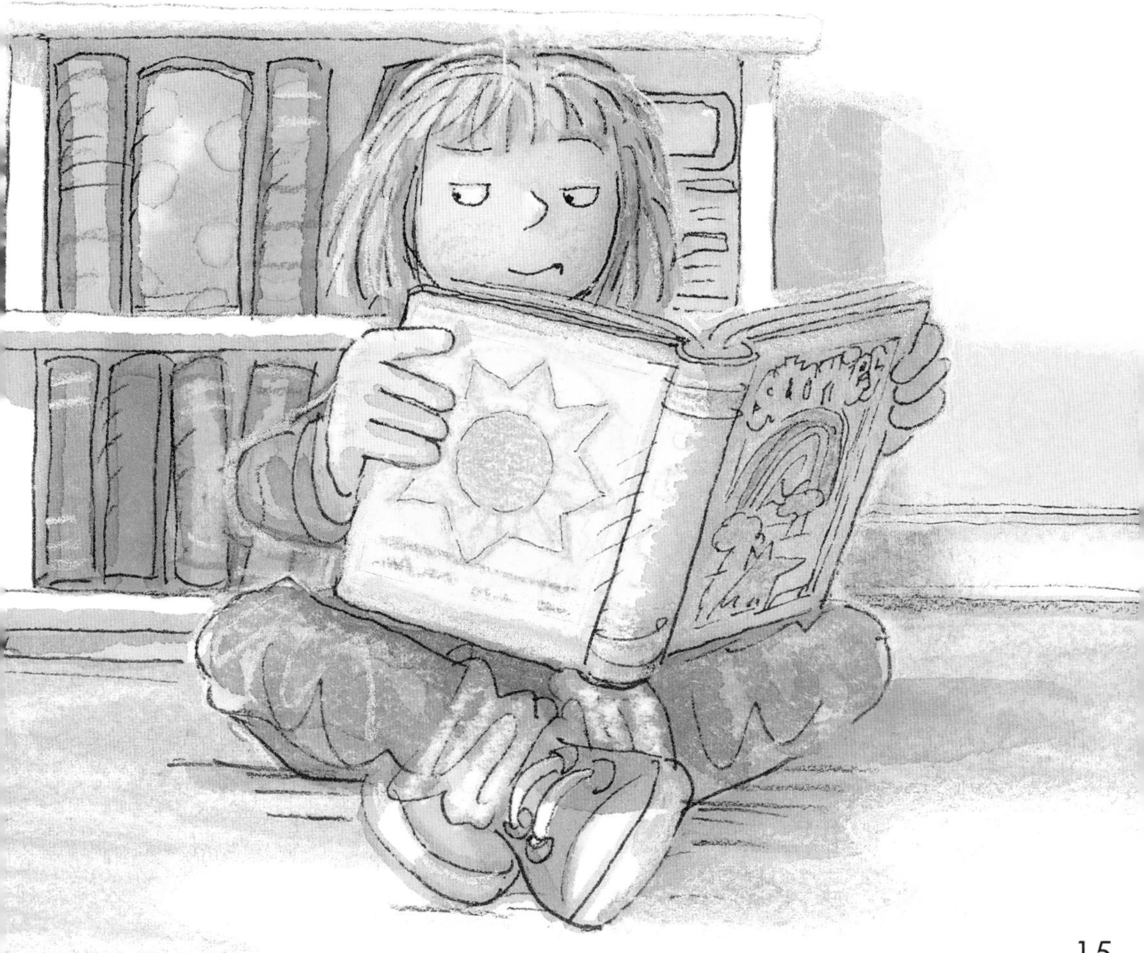

Bobbie says, “Yes, baby. Look!”

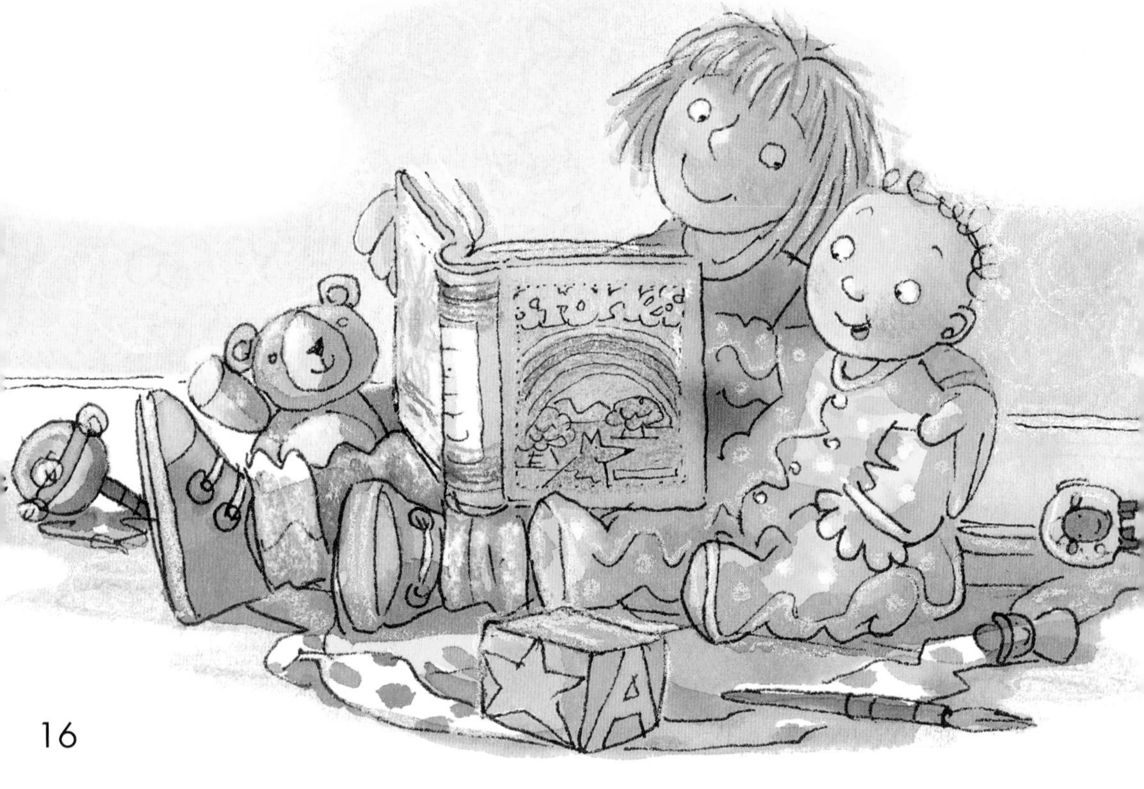